the Blue Room
—— POEMS ——

Carlo Spinazzola

CAPE BRETON UNIVERSITY PRESS
SYDNEY, NOVA SCOTIA

Copyright © 2013 Cape Breton University Press

All rights reserved. No part of this work may be reproduced or used in any form or by any means, electronic or mechanical, including photocopying, recording or any information storage or retrieval system, without the prior written permission of the publisher.

Cape Breton University Press recognizes the support of the Province of Nova Scotia, through the Department of Tourism, Culture and Heritage and the support received for its publishing program from the Canada Council's Block Grants Program. We are pleased to work in partnership with these bodies to develop and promote our cultural resources.

Tourism, Culture and Heritage

Canada Council for the Arts   Conseil des Arts du Canada

Cover design by Cathy MacLean Design, Chéticamp, NS.
Cover image and all other artwork by Carlo Spinazzola.
Layout by Laura Bast, Sydney, NS.
First printed in Canada.

Spinazzola, Carlo, 1970-2003
[Poems. Selections]
    The blue room : poems / Carlo Spinazzola (1970-2003).
ISBN 978-1-927492-51-2 (pbk.)
ISBN 978-1-927492-52-9 (web pdf.)
ISBN 978-1-927492-53-6 (epub.)
ISBN 978-1-927492-54-3 (mobi.)

    I. Title.

PS8637.P56A6 2013   C811'.6   C2013-903770-5

Cape Breton University Press
PO Box 5300
1250 Grand Lake Road
Sydney, Nova Scotia
Canada B1P 6L2
www.cbupress.ca

CONTENTS

Acknowledgements	v
Editor's Note	vi
Foreword	vii
The Blue Room	
Her Shores	2
Albergo Fenestera	3
Strange Reflection	5
Dream	6
Little She	7
In Passing	7
Put All Questions	9
Great Love	10
All I Know	11
Twist	12
All the Stillness	13
Thoughts	14
Drifter	15
Dead	16
The Bus Stop Lady	17
Time To Go Back	17
Bubbles	18
Drunken Gardens	19
Stand Strong	28
Morley Rd.	29
Walter	30
Great Will	32
Exchange #17	34
Words	35
Mistaken	36
From a Window	38
Eat What is Offered	39
Secret Mind	40
Ashley	41
What's the News?	42
Silence of Wholeness	42
Alter	43
Black Crow Stop Sign	45

I've Written for the Drunkard	46
Float	47
Poem	48
Second Cup	50
Jazz Tent	52
Innuendo	53
The Camp	54
Blue Room	55
Horizon	56
Amos	57
To My Fighters	58
Unaware	59
Nothing	59
Sun	67
Peter	68
Beautiful Fool	69
Consummation	72
Thief	72
Aaron's Song	73
Moves Me	74
Iron Lady	75
Cabin Snow Song	76
Lynda	77
Hitching Girls	78
Summer Jazz	79
Caressing Untamed	80
James	81
Release	82
Prayer for His Safe Return	83
Write Me Slowly	84
Silence of Wholeness	85
Old Ways	86
These Words Are Collecting	88
Riding	89
You Who Wage the Tiny Wars	90
Fundamental Simplicity	91
Artist Statement	94
About the Author	95

ACKNOWLEDGEMENTS

Wow! What a ride this project has been. Many doors have opened and many old friendships have been retouched by the expressions of Carlo. That seems to be the way he works even now.

Carlo was the type of person who would give away all he had, asking nothing in return – that was just who he was. Now, his giving is coming around again. In this book, Carlo's works have been made available by the very people who accepted his offerings all those years ago and who continue to hold them close, protecting his expressions and keeping them sacred. This book was an unfulfilled dream of my brother's. Now – ten years after his departure – it has come to fruition. As a result of this journey, I see my brother in a different light and understand him in a much deeper way. For this I am grateful. Thank you Carlo for all you have touched – it has turned to gold.

I would like to give hugs to the following people for their contributions to this project in various ways: Otis A. Tomas for his brilliant and articulate foreword. Laura Bast and Mike Hunter at CBU Press for their dedication to and cooperation in this project. Ronald Caplan and Breton Books for replanting the seed.

Anais Spinazzola, Pasquale and Marilyn Spinazzola, Susan Korol, Kenny Boone, Heather MacLeod, Dale John Campbell, Mike Morrison, Scott Brown, Chris Cowper-Smith, Mike Campbell at the Carleton in Halifax, Vaughan Merchant Photography, Jamie Foulds at Soundpark Studios, Max MacDonald and Barb Cameron, Tanya and Tina Marie Reashore, Rob Doublett, Sheppy, Freddy and Gordie at Lakewind Sound, Helen Musial, Christine Mayer, Brian Newcombe, Ed Woodsworth, Kim Kerr, David Mahalik, Kathy MacGuire, Paul MacLellan and Jesse Ferguson, for his poetic insights.

In harmony,
Angelo Spinazzola
www.spinazzola.ca

EDITOR'S NOTE

These poems were collected from notebooks and papers Carlo left behind – some he printed himself; others he handwrote in various notebooks and on loose-leaf pages. Minor edits have been made, especially to the latter, including the addition of minimal punctuation, some changes in capitalization, correction of spelling mistakes, etc.

The images, all untitled and undated, are either from Carlo's notebooks or are paintings that now hang on the walls of friends and admirers all over Cape Breton and Nova Scotia.

CARLO PLAYED THE BLUES...

The blues ran like a river through Carlo's life: a current that rose from a hidden darkness informed all his work, and finally carried him onward to that ocean of release and freedom he tried to catch a glimpse of all along. When he sat down to play his open-tuned guitar, finger picking a classic blues line or running up the strings with his "bottleneck" slide, his voice rising from a growl to a howl, you might think you were listening to some old-time bluesman from the Mississippi Delta rather than a Cape Breton boy with an Italian name. But the authenticity of Carlo's blues was not based just on his learned musical stylings – it came from a familiarity with the real roots of the blues: a suffering deep in the soul, and a calling for its release.

Though music was closest to his heart, Carlo was more than just a musician. He was a poet, a sculptor, a craftsman, a silversmith, a painter, a woodworker, a teacher, an athlete, a gypsy and more. But just as any real bluesman will tell you that the blues is more than just a musical form – it is the expression of a life intimate with suffering – Carlo's blues found expression in all facets of his life and work. His poetry, his music and his art reflect one another; the spirit of the blues moves behind them all.

As a poet, his words often became his songs, but they took a step beyond the conventional form and style of the typical blues lyrics. Throughout his work, Carlo wants to take us by the hand to show us the hole in the middle of the world where the blues finds its wellspring. He shows us a life lived in the awareness of the aching need that most of us prefer to spend our lives looking away from – a preoccupation with the pain of existence does not help with the day-to-day affairs of providing for our material comforts. It is the role of the tragic artist ("tragedy" being just an older and more respectable name for the blues) to look deeply into the heart of suffering in order to transform it, to make it human and give it a beauty that we can live with. The blues may be a 20th-century musical form, but the sensibility it expresses is universal, and goes back to the beginnings of art. The ancient tragedians knew the blues when their heroes stared into the abyss of an indifferent fate – even the gods were powerless before it. Born into a world where our desires for life and love, pleasure and pride are so quickly subsumed by exploitation and repression, the blues expresses our helplessness while at the same time offering release. We look into the darkness to try to see through to the other side.

In his writing, Carlo takes us into the heart of the blues. He invites us into a world lived in the margins. At one point, he had a tentative title for a collection of some of his poems: *Gift to the Gutter*, as if to express a desire to strip away the pretenses of civility to reveal its core, which under his penetrating gaze might be based in injustice, predation and violence. But, at the same time, the poetry was a gift for those innocents left on the outside, a longing for simplicity. We find here a sympathy for the outcast who, by his very position on the outskirts of society lives closer to the naked truth. Rather than dwelling on the surface, Carlo tells us to

> Keep on tearing to the core
> We all must cling at something
> Our souls tell us that there is more. (p.2)

And he beckons us to

> Step beyond logic
> into
> Fundamental simplicity. (p.91)

Carlo wants us to strip away the conventions by which we hide from our own longings, probing for the unvarnished truth of what really moves us. Somewhere beyond the banal hypocrisies that enable our lives to glide easily over the surface, Carlo found darker truths that he could not turn away from – the pain of mortality, longing, an ache deep in the soul. But at the same time a hint of a deeper truth promises to resolve the loneliness of the self – a salvation, a freedom, a better world; all of this is what is captured in the howl and moan of his blues.

His poetry spans the range of experience from seedy encounters with late-night hookers, where the indifference of the world has turned even love into a commodity, to a hunger for mystical resolution where revelation is felt, awaiting discovery just behind the darkness. Many of his poems are personal, inward reflections, always conscious of the shortcomings revealed when we contemplate a more ideal world. Even love is always tinged with inadequacy. There is always complexity; nothing is as simple as we would like. Even in a more hopeful poem, such as "Put All Questions," which hints at a final unveiling that awaits us, we can't forget that even here

> perfect truth courts
> The lie. (p.9)

Broad and powerful talents come as a gift to some, but gifts often demand compensation. The blues comes as both a blessing and a curse. Carlo was troubled by dark thoughts; it was through his art that he fought his inner battles, and there he looked for glimpses of a freedom that can break through the cages that build up around our lives. He must have known his time was short. His work is pervaded with the sense of need and urgency with which he lived his life. We sense him searching for the freedom that art provides. We see him wrestling with his demons in the powerful and dark imagery, the longing for release, and the tempting of fate to offer up that last glimpse of a truth that can sweep away the loneliness of waiting here below. His writing glows with a fiery intensity that comes only from acknowledgment of the darkness – the shadows serve to accentuate the light, but the light always feels a mysterious threat. We have a sense of something foreboding just below the surface: the artist is compelled to look, even knowing that it might be better to leave well enough alone. Carlo's gifts and his inner demons spurred one another toward their inevitable conclusion.

To get a sense of the significance of Carlo's work, it is important to see it in the context of the full breadth of the artistic undertakings he applied himself to. To see him as just a poet, or a musician, or a painter, is to miss the spirit that ran through all his work. He was all of these things at once – rather than undertaking a rigorous study of any one discipline, his artistic output flowed naturally, taking any number of forms, but always expressing the same spirit. In an interview with *Radio Atlantica*, he said "it doesn't matter what the medium is – it's all in terms of the expression." His life and his work spoke the same message, and this gave all of his endeavours a depth, commitment and truthfulness that is unmistakable.

We can see traces of Carlo's main concerns and styles through the range of his work. His writing is reflected in his songs; his music is reflected in his painting. There is a series of paintings presenting us with scenes of late-night, after-hours sessions in smoky bars – musicians caught in the act of creation, shouting out a midnight freedom from the smoky stages of their late-night cabarets. We see here the exaggerated contortions and soul-wrenching catharsis of a passionate blues singer. His portraits exhibit a rough, direct and expressive folk style, somewhere between caricature and a deep expressionism. Reminiscent of Picasso's "blue period," his palette tends toward the blues as well: note the reclining nude figure painted entirely in blue (p.64). Another painting shows us the artist himself – at work standing before his easel – his head like a block and striking the pose of a triumphant fighter: the artist as hero, conquering the world of unforgiving fate with an act of free creation (p.25).

Carlo didn't just paint or write from an observational standpoint. He fully participated in the life he depicted: he walked the walk. He took his blues seriously; as an emblem of his commitment to the blues, at one point, he even once had burned into his flesh, with a red hot wire, the word "Blue."

In his music and art, as well as in his life, Carlo valued most of all freedom and spontaneity. This was the antidote and self-overcoming of the blues. It was the creative act that could give release. His raw improvisational blues style, echoing the great Delta blues players, cared not for practice and polish. His second recorded album, *Walk*, was recorded and mixed in the studio in one eight-hour session – as if to leave no room for extraneous critical afterthought that might come between the artist and the purity of the moment.

In his painting, perhaps his most striking work is a series of large canvases he painted by arranging them in a circle around several cans of paint, in the centre of which he placed a stick of dynamite – opening to pure spontaneity, to chance and freedom, dealing with fate on equal terms. In one explosive second, the canvases were thus "exposed with an instant of creation," revealing a mystery that stands as a microcosm to the images of the early creative energy of our universe brought to us by the Hubble telescope. Painting with dynamite was characteristic of the immediacy with which Carlo sought experience. It pushed him into unpredictability and to the point of danger: courting risk, exposing himself to chance and fate, seeking that pure instant between the cracks of our rigid world of convention and habit where we can find our true freedom.

> Can you hear the sounds of nothing's explosions
> The popping bubbles of the mind
>
> How to create with these little glances into infinity
> Seems to be the artist's seducing preoccupation.
> (p.47)

The times when he is most free from his darkness are when he is faced with innocence of childhood. There is nostalgia here for a time before the corruption of the world made its demands.

He writes,

> Bring the children in
> Tell them to gather around
> And play in the ideas
> I will watch and learn
> To float again. (p.47)

And:

> Go back to the children
> Remember their eyes
> There was only beauty then
> Wildly helpless without the need for protection.
> (p.80)

He hearkens back to a purity and a remembrance that awaits rediscovery, that is lost in the act of making the necessary compromises of the grown-up world. For Carlo, art is where this original purity can be preserved. Carlo did not merely contemplate within himself these thoughts. He also worked to keep his vision alive through others. He worked, on and off, as a teacher, spending time in the schools of Cape Breton, but more especially, giving his time serving as the cultural director of the Dene Tha Community School on the Chetah reserve in remote Northern Alberta, where he did much to inspire his Aboriginal students (themselves at risk of succumbing and becoming marginalized) in maintaining their pride and identity through the ways of art and creativity.

In the end, Carlo succumbed to his demons. In 2003 the blues carried him away at the age of thirty-three. Whether his inner torments instigated his creativity or were the necessary payment exacted for his gifts is a moot point. Today we are tempted to treat the blues as a medical condition, to be medicated away. Indeed, perhaps something could have intervened between Carlo and his demons. But perhaps, too, we would have lost that source or inevitable compensation for his creative genius. Whatever we may think of that, we wish the price was not so high. But Carlo and his blues lived together, and together they created for us a powerful legacy of words, music, art and memory.

Otis A. Tomas

HER SHORES

Out here in these mountains
You can feel your own mind
Never could though the neon
Always been the lonely kind

Still he swears he will set himself free
Keep on tearing to the core
We all must dig at something
Our souls tell us that there is more

So fill up all your senses
Feel the truth along her shores
Call out across her waters
Embrace each swell that roars
On her shores

He said,
It's been told before
But please let me swear again
It's the brine of the salt seas
That's filling up my veins

Even jagged glass she'll softly smooth
Your dirt she'll carry away
It's the true blue of these waters
That are begging all to stay
On her shores

ALBERGO FENESTERA

By holy Mary hung above his bed
By the child quiet in her arms
By the plaster hanging crucified
By mother's fears for child's harm
I swear now by the dawning

By the aching lovers before us
By all of the pain of passion's end
By these clammy sheets that must accept
The misdelivered gifts I'll send
I swear now by the dawning

By the warmth of her sleeping embrace
By the perfect breast on which I now lay
By the sting of the Kewatian winds
By all of the darkness of its day
I swear now by the dawning

By the promise of morning shadow
By this desk's brick wall view
By the blood red wine
That has stirred the song
Seeping into morning new
I swear now by the dawning

By the cloth hung worn limb dry
By the sweat and grit since passed
By the holes in the souls
That have carried us here
As the first was once the last
I swear now by the dawning

By the silent arms left reaching
By the emptiness of our lies
By the ink scratched here in my chest
By all of the truth that it implies
I swear now by this dawning
Solemn journeys for this new day

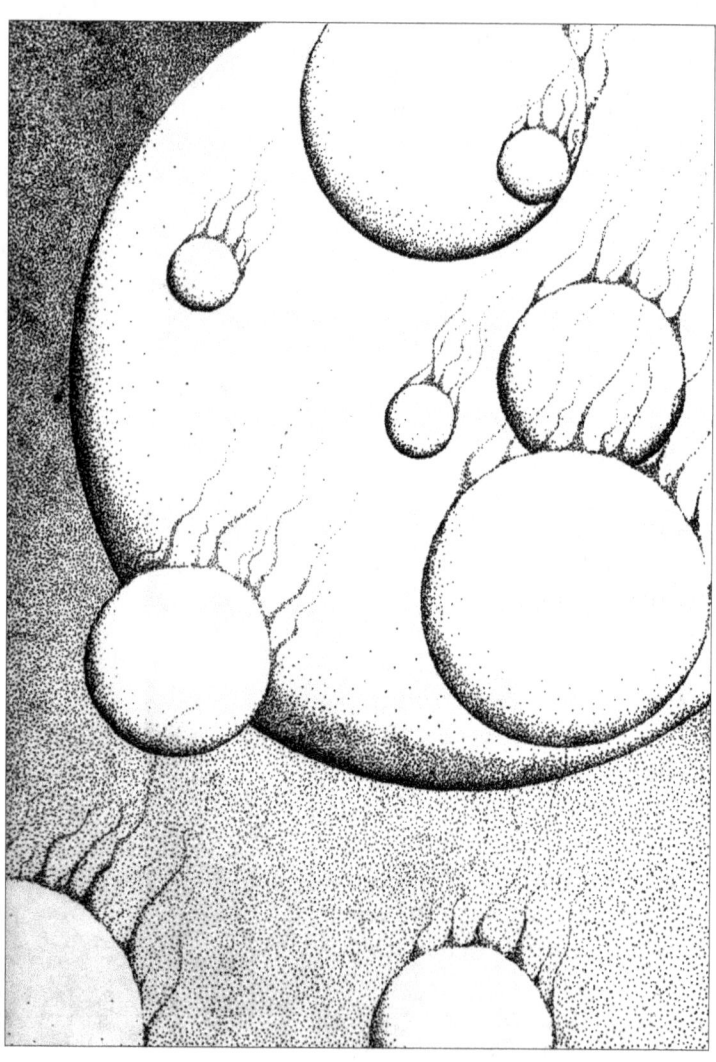

STRANGE REFLECTION

So now what comfort can I find
Lost there inside some other's mind

I don't recognize it
(or myself it seems a strange reflection)

It may be spoken still untrue
We must stand outside the things we do

Been staring down my nose again
Have I forgotten where I have been?
Oh no
So strange

Hold the mind, cup the hands
Gotta get the feet where others stand

So rich by all I have got
Still I stand pauper poor by all I am not

DREAM

Since the smoke has cleared
The lovers' sea has stilled
The fog's dreams
while
Riding naked slow
Through the clear night
Straight into the moon

The hazy dark mist
Is carried sleeping to my bed

Again I awake on the water

LITTLE SHE

Little She is fragile
White crystal porcelain
She seems so lost there
In her ghostly pale skin

Little She of aqua eyes
Sits watching summer's rain
Waiting for the winter's snow
To cover her again

IN PASSING

How many brief solicitations
exist along this noon lane?

How impossibly infinite
Detection comes to pass
In the perspective maze
Of teetering egos and
Incidental swells of emotion

What is your searchlight headline?

Can you guess enough
Strength to raise up your chin?
You will again
Be led back to the memory
Of that perfect child grin
That will multiply with your own

PUT ALL QUESTIONS

Put all questions
To the jury
Of time

And wait

As sure as the passing
The answer will come

As perfect as change
As clear as magic

When the final unveiling
Frees the mass to empty eyes
The unknown will open
With the union

The perfect truth courts
The lie

Great Love
Polarity; out
Far & hard
Has two directions

—Spin.

ALL I KNOW

These moments of uncertainty
That seem to wedge between you and me
Shake the foundations of all I know.
Ain't it clever how the morning sun
Exposes all the lonely ones
Like an undetected teardrop in a circus show?

Chasing myself round the room
Full moon grins from in the gloom
Night leaks stains onto the bathroom floor
In the corner she sways quietly
Bent as an old willow tree
She loves the way that I kick down the door

She was born with the cancer
Of twenty gypsy dancers,
Talks of clouds and rain drops when she's high.
If I could once get under
To dance inside her thunder,
I would bring back lightning from her skies.

TWIST

Twist smoke
Twist words
Twist glances

Anything you choose

Twist until the light squeezes out the ends

Hold dearly this distortion

For relief and a perfect tale
Shape your untwisting
While giving great weight to exchange

All the stillness
Of the infinate
     motion
keeps my deralectic
Bines out on this Ocean.
                    -spin.

THOUGHTS

Thoughts need punctuation
like sentences need words

We need to know the end is near
so we can live inside our fears

Borders of fear
Punctuate
All
Lives

DRIFTER

She is such a wee drifter
Her sheets are woven
Strands of hope and hate
Her pillow is the memory

The bed lay unmade
Her defeat to break the day
She and an old stuffed toy
Permanently distort
The passing

She seeks out the uninterested
Then begs for answers
Too beautiful to be denied
Too sad to understand

Only the big boys get her home
She fucks well
When she feels
Free inside questions need

DEAD

Thinking through getting dead

Is the finite instance of death, not rebirth
Let me propose a moment's motion
These borderlines
Are our disciplines
With or without
We target freedoms
That can only be found at the edges
Out in all direction
Pure and painful

What ugly creature do you fear
Whisper up the image to examine
Seduce and consummate the god illusion
This new-born death becomes
Another piece in this great mystery

Present all to all
Gentle exists in each storm
When spirit dictates survival

The bus stop lady
In dew rag hair
Has sugar ray smiles
And
A kitty KAT
STARE.

—Spin.

Time to go back
Child take me home
Toss your kisses
To the wind.

—Spin.

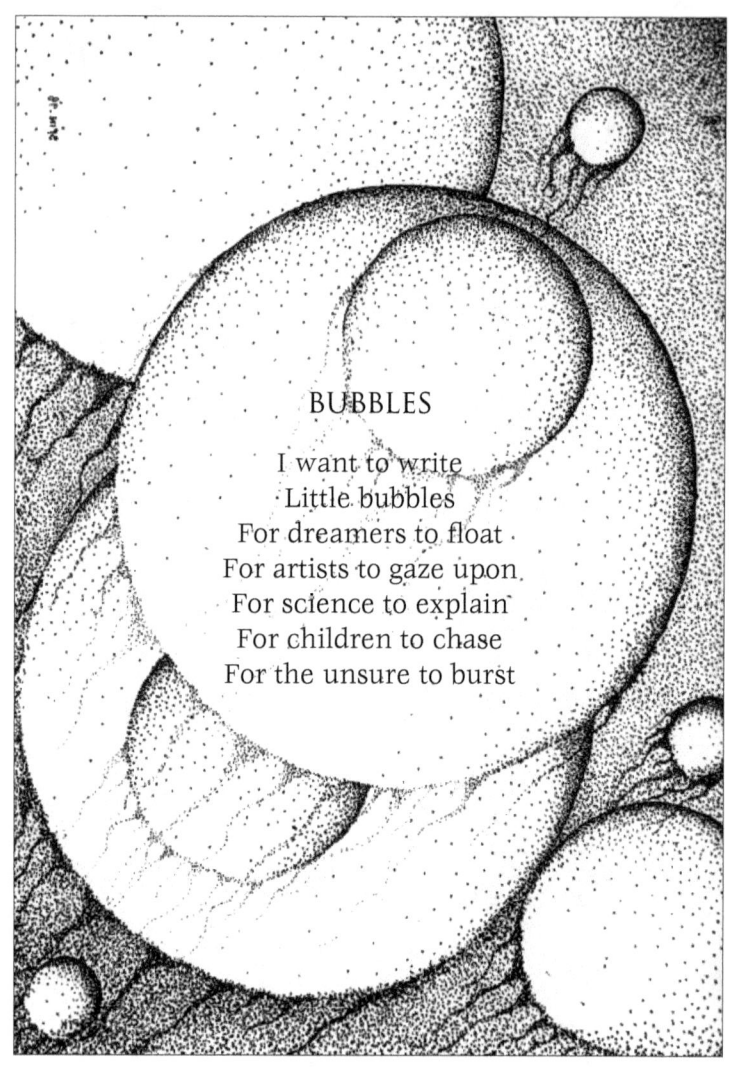

BUBBLES

I want to write
Little bubbles
For dreamers to float
For artists to gaze upon
For science to explain
For children to chase
For the unsure to burst

DRUNKEN GARDENS

Don't get me wrong
Not far from here
Something more exists

Conviction and Delusion
Become conscious thought

Look away
Look away
So glad you couldn't stay

Take the clock down from the wall
Internal rhyme decanters
Serve feasts to a passive hunger

Feed yourself on all hunger
There is much for all

Sleep now in this thunder
Put your wishes in the ground
All your planted seeds
Promise dream lightning

Grow drunken gardens

STAND STRONG

Every second
We generate a scene
In our heads

(stand strong)

If a large one arises
On the outside

(stand strong)

It then becomes our own

Effect and Affect

(stand strong)

Destroy Self

(stand strong)

Close your eyes again
Look inside

(stand strong)

Let the Kings and castles fall

(stand strong)

Gently

MORLEY RD.

Can't find my way to the Morley Rd.
Hope these wheels can carry this load
Gettin' my work done, gettin' stoned
Jesus don't you carry me home
'Cause I'd rather do this thing alone
As I find my way to the Morley Rd.

Wind my way up to the Morley Rd.
Can't help but feel I'm going too slow
Spinning my tail and through snow
Hope these wheels can carry me home
Saint Christopher keeps throwin' them bones
As I wind my way on the Morley Rd.

Moon is risin' as I crest the hill
Thinkin' I might just make it still
Sun is perched just like a crow
The island spreads itself below
Now the sun just hopped off its tree
And my baby waits at home for me

Wind my way down the Morley Rd.
Guess these wheels could carry this load
Only a few more miles to go
The gun has sunk into its glow
The pinhole stars they start to show
My baby waits for me at home
As I find my way on the Morley Rd.

WALTER

These afflictions you've taken on
Let the hollowed souls look invisibly through
The situation is new
Not young

So many in the mists
Famous distortionists

They fear your clarity
Colour inside
Tone inside
Hues inside
This
Genderless
Black
Vessel

They use energy
You channel
Leaving no wake

Expand or doubt as the need serves
You are all given this infinity
He will tell you
If you listen
The Angel man said it's so

(I've even peeked inside)

Sublime understatements
Perfectly balanced
Constantly in motion
Inverting
Imploding

Welcoming all change

Moving through without wake
Few are the numbers as the journey goes on

I believe
Walter is one

GREAT WILL

The summer parks in the city
Always make him helpless
The golden beauties sit in rows
One million miles long
One million smiles away

Stand here by me, statue
I have this poem that has been closing forever
I can't bear to see it close

How do they touch you?

His great granite mind kept pace
And although his worn uniform was militant
He held an Artist's gaze

They touch his cold legs
Whispered drunken secrets

Then more alone

Some would use his altar as a midnight love prop
Spilling abandoned words out
Over the wrinkles of hiked skirt bliss
Shirt draped over bootstrap

You are indeed a man of great will

The lonely dancers close the clubs
Collect the coins
To leave a bit or two there
For the tooth fairy hobos
To rest atop
To ease the sleep

You are indeed a man of great will

The whores' cursing swell
Reminds him of the old victories
In some strange new sand of time

We shared most of the day
With an entire bottle of smoky words

To please the night,
The sun came in and warmed thoughts
To tuck us away in numb statue's sleep

EXCHANGE #17

I found myself moaning
A low whining surrender
Not at
But for
Each passing princess and doormat alike

Playfully I was called out
By these wondrous blue eyes,

"You okay?"

I gave best effort
Calling up a non-intense
"I'm fine" return
But had crumbled in her wake
Long before reaching centre

She gave mercy in a second glance

Without measurable regret
She reached over to pat the moaner's bowed head

As she moved back into the masses
I swear she was purring

WORDS

Words are tools too blunt

Can we reflect what we have not?
Can we remember all forgot?
Can we touch who does not feel?
Can we receive all we steal?

Words can sooth us until emotion understands

You can

MISTAKEN

I might be mistaken
Could well have been the wine
When the shadow of another
Came sneaking up behind

Might be mistaken
Lost inside the rhyme
Was it the black top whisper
Let me listen one more time

Swear I'm short on madness
Running just a bit of spite
Might be mistaken
I ain't loving on you tonight

Seems you came right in
Put your kiss all down my face
Might be mistaken
Cause you ain't left a trace

Might be mistaken
Wish I was a holy man
So I could ask some other
To guide these shaking hands

FROM A WINDOW

Jazz cafés shoe shop cool
All of these accented words
Make a language foreign to sound itself

These creatures seem to understand
How early years cast shadows through light

Clarification of identity
Will thicken the plot in the linear mind

There is intrigue and confusion looking in

Put yourself out there
Look back at the naughty bliss
Filling the empty rooms

Seek out the faces who have let go
If you've gone out truly
You will recognize your own vessel

EAT WHAT IS OFFERED

Eat what is offered
Stuff it in if necessary
Make no apology
Eat your anger

This oozing rage
Is deep inside all

Invert its polarity
Use all of the mysteries
To shape positivity
Carve backward

There are no untouchables

Vomit bile
Drink spittle
Fuck the dead
Eat what is offered

SECRET MIND

Solemn quiet place
Roll it over in your mind
Pacify yourself
Think of a better time

Try to hold it back
Will that keep you here?
Whisper to yourself
Taste the bitter tear

Roll it over in your mind

Sit down beside yourself
Search the words to say
Burnt out memories
Laughing dreams
Screams from yesterday

In you, secret mind
There is nothing left to hide behind
In you, secret mind

Call out to the maker
Spit towards the skies
Pounding sand on your knees
Wipe it from your eyes

ASHLEY

Profane Celtic rapper

Vanity and profanity

Numb from the neck up

Patting foot outward
Feeling for that Columbus line

Never leaving
Already gone

We sat for dinner
I needed him
Just then

Gentle swells of polite confusion
Peeked out

Almost safe
From the mad world of mime

The little peepers gave quiet thanks to his cheap mirror shades

As I monitored my misunderstanding
And checked my nose

WHAT'S THE NEWS?

What's the news? Barnyards, smoke and dreams,
Candles in stone, a very good friend, a huge
Crazy beard of coal, kitchen stove tunes.
I'll fill the page with weak wilting words.
If we go into the depths does it become
Only dark? There must be more on
the edges of your soul hollowed, dredged
By the needs of mars and venus;
Can we ever understand words from
The lurking jaws of our pasts
Handing like the wet cloth of labour,
Woven and driven as day?

Baby Blue the colour has faded slow.
Bring peace to us now, slip
out of the knotted hard night,
Embrace our embrace,
The pain of my disgrace
Draws tight,
Pulls the colours fading into blue baby.

SILENCE OF WHOLENESS

Silence of wholeness
Not a sword or pen
But the sound of quiet motion
Level water cools again
—
The breezes near the dawn
Blow the light across the dream
Like the touch of perfect sleep
Near a lover never seen
—
I breathe her into welcome
Like ripples out across a sea
Righteous as the freedom
Her good love welcomes me

ALTER

Alter your state
Choose your poison
Alter your state
Choose your night

Find grand division
Out in any direction
The diamond cutting edges
Are clearest and purest
Both in their madness and logic

Investigate all duality
Pick any bizarre positivity
Sit gracious and amused
Become a student of sincere abuse
If the need proves true
Unravel your eternity

Alter your state
Remove the blinders
They have been placed
But once gone never replaced

Alter your state
Embrace each of your fears
Surrender holds many victories
In this new place

Alter your state

BLACK CROW STOP SIGN

Black crow stop sign
Waiting for life to bleed in
Closes both his eyes
To feel the day go by

I'll not stop now
I've slown
To see your face
Hiding it away
Hiding it away

So when you wonder where I've been
Stand there with your red light grin
I've already let you in
The crow must fly both ways

I'VE WRITTEN FOR THE DRUNKARD

I've written for the drunkard
Coming through the door
With his enemy and lover
Spilling out across the floors
Floors of butts and ashes from
A time of trees to have lost among the cracks and holes

Where do you find your peace inside?
Is there a window? Is there a door?
Are there sounds of bells or hymns?

FLOAT

Can you hear the sounds of nothing's explosions
The popping bubbles of the mind

How to create with these little glances into infinity
Seems to be the artist's seducing preoccupation

Tell me slowly, make me understand

Point clearly
Carve carefully into this blockhead I've chosen
Take the toys out from your dusty corners of youth
Shape your words
Wet the thoughts
Ignore my signals of
Soapy-eyed confusion

I need perspective

Bring the children in
Tell them to gather around
And play in the ideas
I will watch and learn
To float again

POEM

I want the song
The muse is smiling on

Instead
Single-minded flashes
Stare up from coffees
Street light glances

To serve song
Is to wait with words

If you choose
Freely
We can wait together

Let
The beautiful fools charge gently
The frightened fools be threatened
The brave fools challenged
Let the dreaming fools sleep

Soon it is revealed
All are waiting
To filter definitions
Through fear

Savour the moments
These are for you
You alone
The free-minded
You who can connect
Stoplight logic

When revealing truths
There can be no censorship

So I can be
The fearless poet
If you are
A fearless poem

But for now
If the clock allows
Sit near

Later we may share the song

SECOND CUP

Your smoked coffee shop grin
There against the wall
Could never be more bold
Summer seems so cold
My pen is growing old

But will not settle

The hairy man's familiar voice speaks of sleepy motions

The spring action girls drop by for a break
Their laughter grounded in chains
She spoke perfect English with both hands
And chestnut shouldered motion
in
Acrobatic thoughts
Take me into her mind to greet the afternoon

The chubby gal
Dragged her flip-flops
Out into the street
To join the tidal masses

The boys sit with women's pride
Waiting to be recognized
Or tickled by a glance
A streetside romance unfolds

Nestled in her conscious mind
She glances away
Taking my eye
Her face reads
The embarrassed
Blue Bruised
Miniskirt
Thighs

Soon the little girls come
I love their bantering energy

Close to the womb
Nervous as freedom

The boys send their smiles

JAZZ TENT

The numbers I've been using
Would take life along so nicely
Now they seem spiked in shelter
The umbrella still shades and serves
But the math and maps have multiplied
Language bent in groove science

So much to be free
The tent swells in need

Free afternoon recognition of the old-faced Jazzers
Greased slides on the warm wind roll words along

Openings are for proper praise
Supreme support exchanges

The little child needs
No excuse to stare
No reason to smile
No need to count
Or be counted

So many directions
Toward perfect emotion

INNUENDO

I will undress a poem
Unable and unaware
Naked as thought
Unfair as a measure

Burdens of witness unpure
Become context for creation

How many words must be piled
Before recognition of freedom settles

I am yet to meet a beast unfair
Yet to meet a gentle man
We live deep inside this innuendo

We give reluctant growth to decay

Our treasures and their burial
Guarded
Protected
For all to see

Our exhumed ancestors
Invest in a glance
Naked innuendo

The reluctant have grown to fear themselves
They cannot stand to recognize the unveiling

Innuendo's
Purity
is
Shivering in her naked beauty

THE CAMP

Effort and all of its direction is so quickly disbanded
Out here near the Columbus line there can be no resistance
Even the drug store girls
Recognize and retire their restless dreams

Out here

The breathless confusion gives way to the humming of gentle
    gypsy songs

How simple it becomes
Blue water clarity
Washed brook stones
Witness the fiddles dance
Mending melodic mummers
Acceptance of birth's decay
This is where we drink our earth
Surrender thought resistance
There can be no perfect exchange

All are thieves
All misuse trust

Like mad lovers' laughter
Unaware and misunderstood
They balance the fringes with your fears

And as the fire dies
You press out words
I cry for the womb
You offer nothing
Refuse no one

Your caravan eyes float outward forever

BLUE ROOM

Allow me this moment
To step inside your mind's trap

Conceive a colour
Melt it to blue
Bring yourself to allow another in
Together empty the corners
Create space

Now sit in the stark empty walled room
Listen to those blues

Can you touch a deeper place?
Hear her speak

Feel her bend your rules into beat
Pushing
Pulling
Patting
Parades on Paradise

After this visit
You can never unknow
The pure emotion of true soul

HORIZON

After the stage
Deep inside city
The boy hitched out
In search of sky and sea
Mother would say words
To her beads and string to guide him
He would sit at water's edge waiting for the day

This is the healing
That the forgiving

Where the two meet is now a dawning for the boy
So there he would wait as the sleeping boats bobbed

There on one edge of a world looking out dusty grey across the healing
A suspicious crab and a cackling daredevil bird mirror a sunrise line
All of these strange symmetries of sky and sea sensibilities balanced him
If then he thought if the sea the healer and the sky the forgiving
Are they not the same?

To heal is to forgive
To forgive is to heal

Baffled by the duality he allowed his surrender
Again he drifted out as the sun
Rose from a boundless place
He witnessed the marriage
Sky is sea
Sea is sky

Horizons are our creation
Like beads and a string they guide us

AMOS

Deep down

The million dollar sorrow artist
Knows the spirits in the streets
He knows why they've left the land

Still we dare admire the symptoms
While he lives the paradox
Whispering proudly
Through
Inuit eyes
Crows' souls
Arctic spirits

What are you all hiding?
Everything you hold
Has been placed and is sacred

Make yourself open to all exchanges
Out here past the street lamps
Out here past the northern light
There are no homes to house your fears

Amos knows

TO MY FIGHTERS

What sort of mess do your fighters carry?
Isn't this the way to handle rulers?
Take the one that needs you most

They laugh to feed false charity
Personal damage is simply baggage

I suppose care can be taken
But to what place?
To do what?

Frightened glances
Passing
Running

Frenzies searching out
Settling low

There are so many ways to be defeated
Bloody knuckles and frightened gangs
Gather to feast on affirmation
You allow defeat and relief in a moment's notice

Take accusation from your eyes
Redirect the energy

Serve muddy water to tears
Your need is also their fear

Inverted anger can decay hatred

It seems such a pleasure to be frightened
By all of the puppet string fighters inside

UNAWARE

Unaware masses file in
Slaughterhouse style
The free and unacquainted
Mingle with the creatures

Smiling
Poking

Feeding poisons
Pretty as the rains

This sickness was passed
We have fostered it
And nursed its suckling
Into rows of two
Outward from the Ark

NOTHING

Ain't nothin' left for nothin'
Ain't nothin' left no more
Some day you will feel all this cold I'm sure

Late night laughter
Porter's alley
Echoed by the full moon's whores
I'll sleep tight in hobo heaven
Blind drunk outside your door
Ain't nothin' left no more

Let the modern music ring the bells
Pile on the tavern floors
So long young rockers' songs
They've all been sung before
Ain't nothin' left no more

SUN

Caught in midnight
Flash beam

She has blistered
The sky skin
Until the cancer is her healing

The yellow god
Will watch as we kneeling
Followers
Wilt in bunt praise

PETER

There are no friends here
But the faces are kind
I'm not high
But I'm happy
The traffic eats my blues
But there are many gentle ears passing

In the classical cave church
On the south end of this town
Peter sat down for some big room sounds

Earlier he stopped by passing for some blues
Being clearly mad we made quick sense

His crept in as lineage
So of course he explained he was a bear
Although he did not notice I was a crow
This is my note of thanks just the same

Your mind is clean and beautiful

Peter
What was the music's plot
When it helped you uncover
This enormous soul?

BEAUTIFUL FOOL

He had begun to mistake the smells of sex
For intellect

Her words were always enough
In return he would find
A few spare minutes to rush
To her sleeping bedside
To devour her thoughts
Then deeply kiss her mouth
"Taste your beauty" he whispers

Later they meet for coffee
She tells him of her dream morning

With poetic agony she speaks
Of a shivering beautiful fool
Who sleeps on the water
Who wakes in her words
Who drowns in her eyes

CONSUMMATION

So now you buzzard goddess
Is this formal pose your final hunger?

It all sang of sky grace
Only a moment ago

The circling courting this perfect death
The silhouette fed the need

There gazing up at the future
I felt the pure emotion
And for an instant
Shared your ocean sky

Upon descent your whispered wings
Rolled back to expose your ebbed gullet
The beauty broken down
The magical mirage revealed

I offer the eyes first

She posed poised

All filled all

THIEF

There ain't no one home no more
There will be no rest
Tonight
A hippie child stole my crow
She took it from my eyes
The little gypsy thief
That I love past touch
Has my crow

AARON'S SONG

When he'd lost her
He swore he had lost it all
From a darkened corner
He heard his guitar call
So he took her up and held her
As if he was holding you
All that she could sing
Was twelve solid bars in blue

You can still see his face
All hanging around the town
Cold as the steel
On the day they cut him down
When you ask him
Where
He'll say
I just been there
Gonna get back real soon

Fade to black
Fight your way back
Fade to black
Fightin' nothing new
Fade to black
Fightin' all that he can do

Sold all his blues
To the radio man for news
Heard it come back through a grin
Still he can't say who wears the scars
Or tell of how we've gone too far
Funny how it's twisting near the end

MOVES ME

In the way you walk
Said before but it moves me
In the way you talk now
Said before but it moves me

To see you standing at the edge of my bed
Sends the little crazies all shooting through my head
Moves me

To grab just a bit of your attention
Lord knows it moves me
When I hear you talking with your uppity friends
The name gets the mention
That moves me through

To hear your velvet voice
Long distance on the phone
It's enough to make this gypsy
Break his travelling bone
You move me

IRON LADY

We are here inside the grand hall
There is a woman with iron on her legs

Proud
Slow

She moves towards us

All Eyes
Flick
Blink
Twitch
Glance

All but hers

They say
Strength is not a physical measure
Strength is not empathy or sympathy

Strength
is
as
Proud
and
Slow
as
Beauty

CABIN SNOW SONG

Share with me one last cigarette
Just before you go
Maybe a warm cup of coffee
Could take the ice off your freezing cold

Take a look outside the window girl
Snow is dancing around the cabin's door
There's this ringing in my ears
That resonates down to my rotting core

I know that spring is nearly round
But your spirit just won't let you be
All locked inside the bell tower
Spinning yarns with a fool like me

All my fears are trivial
Too trivial to be ignored
I was born a pleaser
Born to be used up dried up
Fucked up and ignored

I see you as the snow
You need to find yourself a quiet place to lay
So undo those fancy buttons on that fancy dress
Lay down and say you'll stay

Maybe it's the fireside
Where you keep your secret voices stored
Or is it on the inside
Where January's fires like your passion roared?

The cigarette is long since gone
I'm staring down at coffee grounds
I can't find it in myself
To beg of you to stay

Now I'll stare through silent window pane
As the snow drags you away

LYNDA

An open-roaded holiday
I'm singing to the sun,
The minstrel gypsy melody,
Dance my little one.

Lynda Fiorinda Ca Lucia,
Lynda Fiorinda Ca Lucia.

Old Quebec,
Morisee Falls,
The day of my birth.

Singing to the smiling faces,
In the oldest part of town,
Later near the river's bed,
I laid your body down.

Just then I was king of all,
Filthy rag as crown,
Wine and flames in your blue eyes,
Against the forest sounds.

Walking in the morning's sun,
Let the cars roll on by,
Can't begin to tell her all,
It would be a crime to try.

Even as I stand today,
My mind wanders there,
To the sweet one's gypsy eyes,
And the summer's sun we shared.

HITCHING GIRLS

They gave gracious gifts that sank into a sandy night mind

The ocean girl in her beauty said:

Asking and wondering
Gives inspiration
Fuel

The smoking intellect said:

Master Navigators
In impossible seas
Make
Destiny

Remember your moons

The third and brightest star
The quick burner
Was lost in elastic time smiles

Over good wine
They gave the gifts of an ocean whisper and a buoy bell

I thanked their spirit constellations with a tattoo in the stars

Thank you for the salty dreams
Thank you for the tide's blessing

Oh how the city can bind us

There is a bent light caressing all we know

Lift the bottle
Make the toast

To all accepted
To all left behind

SUMMER JAZZ

In the lullaby leaves
By the big brass band
She smiles coy and throws out a point
She has a child to dance on her stage

In her mind she writes windy words
As the tuba walks along the charted line gliss
Counting some new four time thing

I've just found out about love

This is her show now
Cameras poke into tent-covered melodies
Fog holds up the heavy air
For the hum singers' grins

CARESSING UNTAMED

At this very instance you caress the untamed
You alone choose to wake the sleeping lion

These crazy naked thoughts that disturb you
Are watching from outside the cage

Through the grey steel enemies

Go back to the children
Remember their eyes
There was only beauty then
Wildly helpless without the need for protection

Constant beginnings give way to the feverish pace

You see yourself there unbridled in awakened dreams
Pushing out the offering without response

You feel primal pulse
Beating intuitive answers

Become the scent now
Look back and see
The lazy kings caged and alone
In the shrinking kingdom

In search of some dreaming rage
Out on the other side of passion

JAMES

James, she pointed out,
He would give it all away
So that his massive gifts of perspective can echo through
The bungled saturated mindscapes

He would wake
pissing on the VCR
Make no claim of understanding
Then offer vague apology grins
Over burnt toast mid-day brunch

One side always impossibly high
The other a fidgeting little boy

He has the perfect curse
Slipping in and out of the reference prayers
Without once sticking in the goop

Constantly erratic
Beautifully broken
Sitting comfortably in the grand garden
While all wait for a fumbling cue

With emotion that gives threat to most
A gentle chosen few
Have the uncanny ability to destroy themselves
With perfect grace

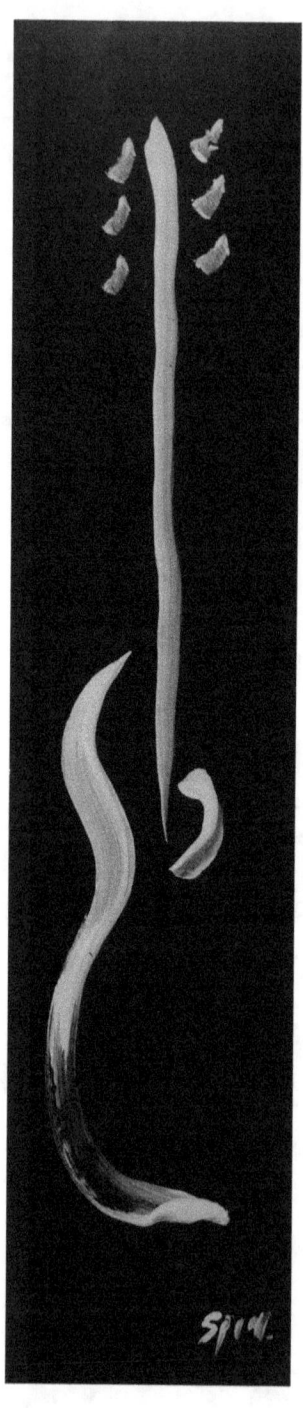

RELEASE

Are we prepared for release?

To allow the proud
To be proud?

The young to be young?

The free to be free?

Have we learned
To celebrate the loss?
To welcome the gains exchanged?

Can we find the infant's eyes
In the old mad man's grin?

Opportunity shares
Space with all

We will reflect
All that we
Cannot accept

PRAYER FOR HIS SAFE RETURN

Everyone must take to the road
Set out to find what they must find
Why should he stand different than me?
That's why I sing this prayer for his safe return

Now when you close brown eyes
Under wide western skies
To let dreams fly
May they be strong and true
As our father's wine, our mother's song
And may you feel this prayer for your safe return

Lord I've watched him grow
I know he's a tender child
So stand by him
Keep him true
Let him hear this prayer for his safe return

WRITE ME SLOWLY

Write me slowly
Use all of the ink
Spend every thought
Press down hard
On the passing pages

Write me in longing
Waiting for the final revealing leaf

Write me freely
Spill over the ink
Some are meant for cleaning

Your complete works will leave
Nothing unwritten
Nothing untouched

SILENCE OF WHOLENESS

Silence of wholeness
Not a sword or pen
But the sound of quiet motion
Level water cools again
—
The breezes near the dawn
Blow the light across the dream
Like the touch of perfect sleep
Near a lover never seen
—
I breathe her into welcome
Like ripples out across a sea
Righteous as the freedom
Her good love welcomes me

OLD WAYS

Take the tea as black as the coal,
She puts it on the night before,
As the salted summer wind blows,
In the rattles of the opened window.

Oh Maggie will you come and dance one for me?
She steps clear across kitchen floor,
McMaster's reel from the radio,
Evening comes in slow,
Eyes closed, laid back, humming low.

Old ways, old ways,
Never let you down they say,
So I'll take it day by day,
It's still the only way I know.

I'll watch from kitchen's glow,
She'll comb her long hair through,
Staring deep past the mirror,
She brushes a tear,
Dims the lamp once more.

Soon the sun will rise again,
Turning quietly as if not for me to see,
She'll draw the bed and fold her hands,
Around worn rosary and pray,
In words for a boy the sea's taken away.

Maggie C., her bow cuts proud,
She breaks the morning's green sea,
Like each morning before,
She'll wave me off from the door,
I'll sing reels to the sea once more.

Clearing harbour, round to French Point,
Nearing the mark, Jacob's head,
I'll drop her engines way down,
Skirt the stern full around,
Sing low laments for the boy taken by the sea.

I will cry here clear off of the shore,
The ears may not be known,
If the sea would cast her spray,
But she lay dead calm today,
Still there is much respect to pay.

THESE WORDS ARE COLLECTING

These words are collecting
My soul is for detecting
You all left behind
Some other understanding
You won't let you find
Your oppression of all
You can't accept
What you cannot find
Is the wind we use
to free you
Nobel Savages
in search of essential words

Riding
 on this
  clear
   night
Straight into the moon.

— Spin.

YOU WHO WAGE THE TINY WARS

You who wage the tiny wars
Defending those tormented,
This balance in your own mind,
Could it be prevented?

You who hold the need so tight
Afraid that they might see you
Circles hidden in the night
Roll down to free you

You're waging that little war again
Twisted and tormented
Laughing at every thing
Tell them everything they know

You who wage those tiny wars
You who can prevent them
You feel for all you know

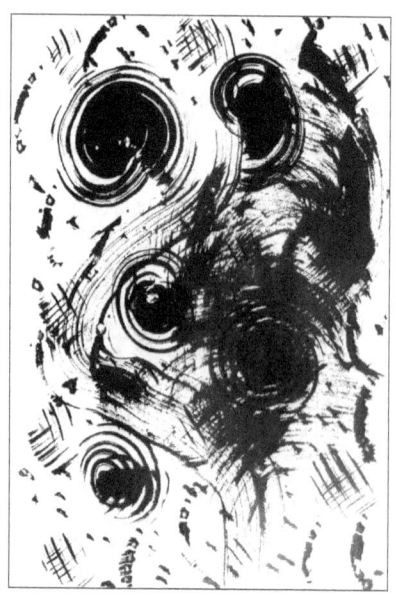

FUNDAMENTAL SIMPLICITY

Step beyond logic
into
Fundamental simplicity

Wear no signs
Carry no sticks or flag
When they say words
Collect cool colours of soul

There can be no need for apology
If the gift falls unnoticed
You can become yourself at the end of this unmeasurable moment
This is the land of the grey where we walk

Please do not forget to dream
Allow it to drape as a backdrop
For each instance of motion
Until there is no resistance

ARTIST STATEMENT

Aritst statement for DeCoNsTrUcTiOn, *solo art exhibition at the Cape Breton University Art Gallery.*

As an artist, I tend to get largely consumed at the onset of a new creative venture, and my pursuits of that goal become the source of what I call "inspirational fuel." All hope and faith is then placed on the observer – you must be prepared to use these gifts as reflective tools. The paintings, the music, the video – these are all simply individual items. In order to maximize their power, you must allow yourself to examine the emotion and spirit of this entire body of materials. In turn, I hope that you can reinvest the intense energy as a positive force in your being.

I consider myself a fine roots artist, primitive in line and colour as well as raw in verse and melody. With this comes the guarded nature and implied grandeur of an artist whose sole purpose is not to be confused by second-guessing while creating. Instead, I try to make the expression complete and then comfortably move on to the next project in waiting. Please enjoy the show and support the arts in your community.

Sincerely,
Carlo Spinazzola
February 19, 2002

CARLO SPINAZZOLA
1970-2003

In the Spinazzola house – family home to parents Marilyn and Pasquale, and children, Carlo and Angelo – there is a blue room. In the blue room Carlo sometimes found inspiration and outlet. After his death, the blue room housed an eclectic array of his art, instruments, notebooks and clippings. To date, the contents of that room have been slowly dispersed to the people Carlo has inspired over the years.

Carlo Spinazzola was an integral part of the Cape Breton art scene during his lifetime. As a songwriter and musician, he wrote, toured and recorded across the Island, province and throughout Canada.

He opened for Colin James and the Little Big Band, Lawrence Gowan, Barney Bentall and the Legendary Hearts, Martin Sexton, The Barra MacNeils and J.P. Cormier, among others. He played in Father John's Medicine Train (1987-1990), Green Eggs and Jam (1989-1995), The Wayouts (1995-1998) and as a solo performer. He recorded three solo albums (*Walk*, *Spinazzola*, *Release*), was nominated for two East Coast Music Awards (Most Promising Artist and Roots Traditional Solo Recording of the year) and co-wrote "All I Know" with his friend and collaborator Gordie Sampson, which can be found on Sampson's *Sunburn* album.

Spinazzola's visual art was featured in the exhibition *DeCoNsTrUcTiOn* at the Cape Breton University Art Gallery; his introduction to the exhibition appears in this volume.

He worked, on and off, as a teacher, spending time in the schools of Cape Breton. In later years – and at the time of his untimely death – Carlo was a teacher in the Dene Tha Community School on the Chetah reserve in remote Northern Alberta. It was a role he enjoyed tremendously.

Carlo was generous beyond words, sharing all that he had. He repaid friendship and kindnesses by sharing pieces of himself – a painting, a found object, a poem. We have left it to Otis A. Tomas, in his poignant foreword to this book, to illuminate the creative life of Carlo Spinazzola.

This book, in a way, now has the same purpose that the blue room once had; it contains some of the art that the room once housed, and it is our hope that the book will continue to inspire people the way Carlo did.

www.ingramcontent.com/pod-product-compliance
Lightning Source LLC
LaVergne TN
LVHW021117080426
835512LV00011B/2552